botanical line drawing:

cacti & succulent edition

200 Step-by-Step Illustrations

by peggy dean

Botanical Line Drawing: Cacti & Succulent Edition
ISBN-10:0-9985585-3-2
ISBN-13:978-0-9985585-3-0

First edition 2017

10 9 8 7 6 5 4 3 2 1

dedicated to
YOU

Welcome to the second edition of Botanical Line Drawing, featuring all of your favorite cacti and succulents! If you've journeyed through my first book on botanical line drawing, then you're probably familiar with the fun art of line drawing. If this is your first time, get ready for some fun!

Line drawing is a playful, sometimes delicate, and easier-than-you-probably-expect art form that doesn't require many materials, but still allows you to branch out and create something gorgeous by applying other types of art to your illustrations. Line drawing looks lovely as a standalone piece, but also works well when incorporating watercolor, hand lettering, etc. Adding line drawing can really bring a piece to life.

This step-by-step book guides you through pages and pages of simple illustrated instruction, introducing 6 steps per illustration. You will see that each step adds onto the shape or detail, and in no time, you'll have produced your very own coveted line drawings!

I encourage you to pull out a sketchbook and practice these flowers separately, then bring them together to showcase terrariums, planters, succulent garden, and more. Options are limitless with this art form!

My favorite pens: Microns 03 & 05
My favorite paper: Moleskine, Rhodia, Canson

let's start!

contents

share your work!

↓

#botanicallinedrawing

---

grab my
other books ↓

cacti

line drawing: cacti & succulents

button cactus

step 1

step 2

step 3

step 4

step 5

step 6

≶ done ≶

draw
it!

line drawing: cacti & succulents

patilion

step 1

step 2

step 3

step 4

step 5

step 6

≷ done ≷

draw it!

line drawing: cacti & succulents

bunny ears

step 1

step 2

step 3

step 4

step 5

step 6

⋛ done ⋚
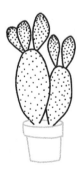

draw it!

line drawing: cacti & succulents

san pedro cactus

step 1

step 2

step 3

step 4

step 5

step 6

≷ done ≷

draw it!

thumb cactus

step 1

step 2

step 3

step 4

step 5

step 6

≥ done ≥

draw it!

line drawing: cacti & succulents
pingpong ball cactus

step 1

step 2

step 3

step 4

step 5

step 6

≷ done ≷

draw it!

line drawing: cacti & succulents
feather cactus

step 1

step 2

step 3

step 4

step 5

step 6

done

draw it!

line drawing: cacti & succulents

notocactus

step 1   **step 2**   **step 3**

step 4   **step 5**   **step 6**

> done

> draw it!

lemon vined

step 1

step 2

step 3

step 4

step 5

step 6

≳ done ≲

draw it!

line drawing: cacti & succulents

dutchmans pipe cactus

step 1

step 2

step 3

step 4

step 5

step 6

≥ done ≤

draw it!

discocactus

step 1

step 2

step 3

step 4

step 5

step 6

⋛ done ⋛

draw it!

line drawing: cacti & succulents

Star rock

step 1

step 2

step 3

step 4

step 5

step 6

≥ done ≤

draw it!

21

line drawing: cacti & succulents

dwarf turk's cap

step 1
step 2
step 3

step 4
step 5
step 6

≥ done ≤

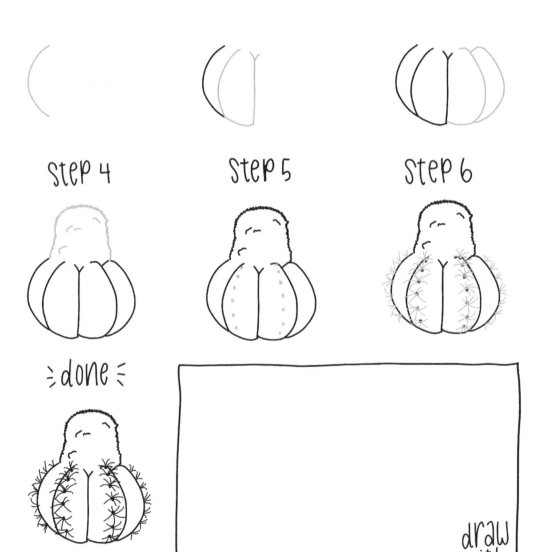

draw it!

line drawing: cacti & succulents

brazilian blue cactus

step 1

step 2

step 3

step 4

step 5

step 6

⋛done⋚

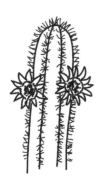

draw it!

23

line drawing: cacti & succulents

blind pear

Step 1

Step 2

Step 3

Step 4

Step 5

Step 6

≥ done ≤

draw it!

line drawing: cacti & succulents

dwarf chin cactus

Step 1

Step 2

Step 3

Step 4

Step 5

Step 6

≷ done ≷

draw
it!

mexican giant cactus

step 1

step 2

step 3

step 4

step 5

step 6

≳ done ≲

draw
it!

line drawing: cacti & succulents

hibotan

step 1

step 2

step 3

step 4

step 5

step 6

≥done≤

draw it!

golden barrel cactus

step 1

step 2

step 3

step 4

step 5

step 6

≥ done ≤

draw
it!

line drawing: cacti & succulents

turtle shell

step 1

step 2

step 3

step 4

step 5

step 6

≷ done ≷

draw it!

line drawing: cacti & succulents

living rock cactus

step 1

step 2

step 3

step 4

step 5

step 6

≈ done ≈

draw it!

line drawing: cacti & succulents

deserts blooming jewel

Step 1

Step 2

Step 3

Step 4

Step 5

Step 6

⋚done⋚

draw it!

little mouse crown cactus

Step 1

Step 2

Step 3

Step 4

Step 5

Step 6

≶ done ≶

draw it!

line drawing: cacti & succulents

spiralis

step 1

step 2

step 3

step 4

step 5

step 6

≥ done ≤

draw
it!

33

line drawing: cacti & succulents

star peyote

step 1

step 2

step 3

step 4

step 5

step 6

≥ done ≤

draw it!

line drawing: cacti & succulents

bleo

step 1

step 2

step 3

step 4

step 5

step 6

≥done≥

draw it!

easter lily cactus

Step 1

Step 2

Step 3

Step 4

Step 5

Step 6

≥ done ≤

draw it!

36

line drawing: cacti & succulents

queen of the night

step 1

step 2

step 3

step 4

step 5

step 6

⋟ done ⋞

draw it!

line drawing: cacti & succulents

whortleberry

step 1

step 2

step 3

step 4

step 5

step 6

≥ done ≈

draw
it!

line drawing: cacti & succulents

mandacaru

step 1

step 2

step 3

step 4

step 5

step 6

≥ done ≤

draw it!

line drawing: cacti & succulents

sea urchin cactus

step 1

step 2

step 3

step 4
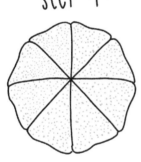

step 5

step 6

≳done≲

draw it!

line drawing: cacti & succulents
elephant cactus

step 1

step 2

step 3

step 4

step 5

step 6

≥ done ≤

draw it!

pink quill

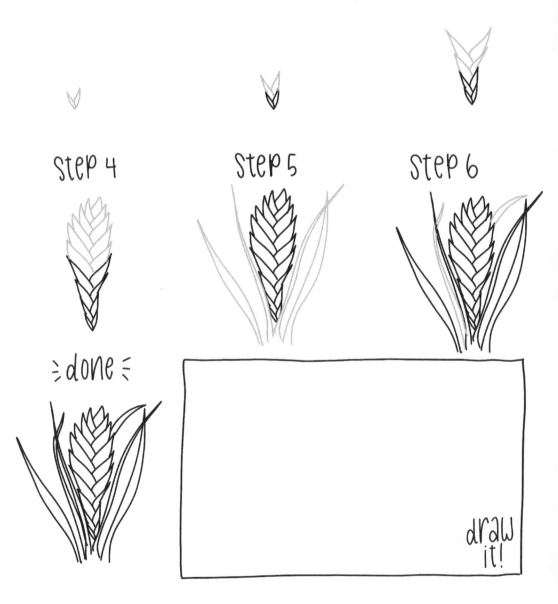

step 1

step 2

step 3

step 4

step 5

step 6

≷ done ≷

draw it!

line drawing: cacti & succulents

pitaya

step 1

step 2

step 3

step 4

step 5

step 6

⋛ done ⋚

draw
it!

line drawing: cacti & succulents

sheep's tongue

step 1

step 2

step 3

step 4

step 5

step 6

≥ done ≤

draw it!

dancing bones cactus

step 1

step 2

step 3

step 4

step 5

step 6

≶ done ≶

draw
it!

45

line drawing: cacti & succulents

woodlouse cactus

Step 1

Step 2

Step 3

Step 4

Step 5

Step 6

≷ done ≷

draw
it!

line drawing: cacti & succulents

perrito

step 1

step 2

step 3

step 4

step 5

step 6

≶ done ≶

draw it!

line drawing: cacti & succulents

torch cactus

step 1

step 2

step 3

step 4

step 5

step 6

≥ done ≤

draw it!

48

line drawing: cacti & succulents

apple cactus

step 1

step 2

step 3

step 4

step 5

step 6

⋛ done ⋚

draw it!

line drawing: cacti & succulents

orange snowball

Step 1

Step 2

Step 3

Step 4

Step 5

Step 6

⋛ done ⋚

draw
it!

prickly pear

step 1

step 2

step 3

step 4

step 5

step 6

≥ done ≤

draw it!

pine cone cactus

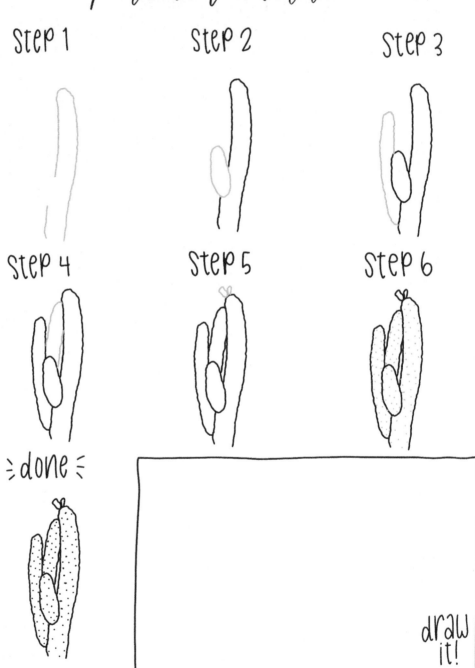

step 1

step 2

step 3

step 4

step 5

step 6

≥ done ≤

draw it!

line drawing: cacti & succulents

fairy castle cactus

step 1

step 2

step 3

step 4

step 5

step 6

≷ done ≷

draw it!

paddle cactus

step 1

step 2

step 3

step 4

step 5

step 6

≥ done ≥

draw it!

line drawing: cacti & succulents

lobivia

Step 1

Step 2

Step 3

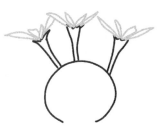

Step 4

Step 5

Step 6

≷ done ≷

draw it!

line drawing: cacti & succulents

crested blue flame

step 1

step 2

step 3

step 4

step 5

step 6

done

draw it!

bottle cactus

step 1

step 2

step 3

step 4

step 5

step 6

≶ done ≶

draw it!

line drawing: cacti & succulents

lemon ball cactus

step 1

step 2

step 3

step 4

step 5

step 6

≥ done ≤

draw it!

line drawing: cacti & succulents

snow white

STEP 1
STEP 2
STEP 3
STEP 4
STEP 5
STEP 6

≥ done ≥

draw
it!

line drawing: cacti & succulents

toothpick cactus

step 1

step 2
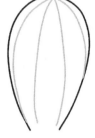

step 3

step 4
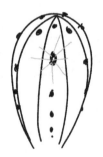

step 5

step 6
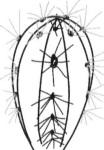

·done·
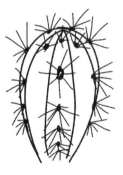

draw
it!

line drawing: cacti & succulents

wheel cactus

Step 1

Step 2

Step 3

Step 4

Step 5

Step 6

≥ done ≥

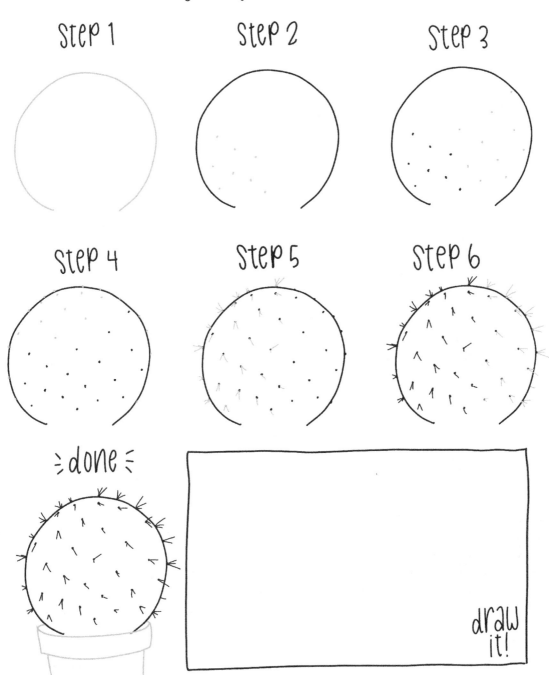

draw it!

line drawing: cacti & succulents

dog tail cactus

Step 1

Step 2

Step 3

step 4

Step 5

step 6

≥ done ≤

draw
it!

line drawing: cacti & succulents

eve's needle

step 1

step 2

step 3

step 4

step 5

step 6

≥ done ≤

draw
it!

63

line drawing: cacti & succulents

percy cactus

step 1

step 2

step 3

step 4

step 5

step 6

≷ done ≷

draw it!

line drawing: cacti & succulents

breast cactus

step 1

step 2

step 3

step 4

step 5

step 6

≶ done ≶

draw it!

peruvian apple cactus

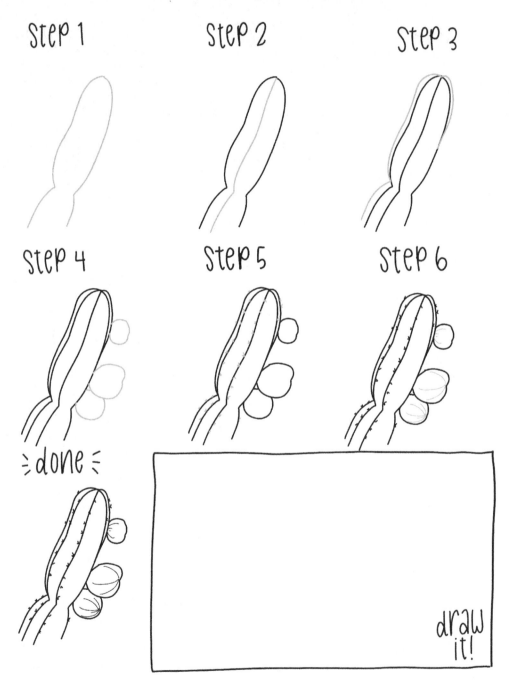

step 1

step 2

step 3

step 4

step 5

step 6

≥ done ≤

draw it!

line drawing: cacti & succulents

cardon

step 1

step 2

step 3

step 4

step 5

step 6

≥ done ≤

draw it!

baseball bat cactus

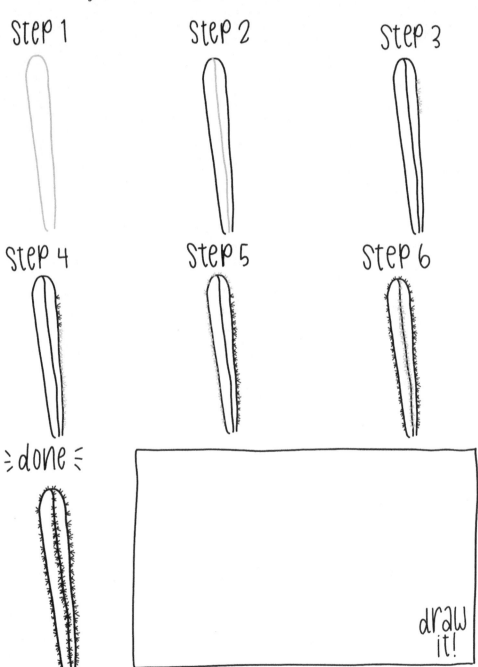

step 1

step 2

step 3

step 4

step 5

step 6

≥done≤

draw it!

line drawing: cacti & succulents

dragon fruit

step 1

step 2

step 3

step 4

step 5

step 6

≥ done ≥

draw it!

artichoke cactus

step 1

step 2

step 3

step 4

step 5

step 6

≥ done ≥

draw it!

line drawing: cacti & succulents

barbora

step 1

step 2

step 3

step 4

step 5

step 6

≷ done ≷

draw
it!

line drawing: cacti & succulents

zygocactus

Step 1

Step 2

Step 3

Step 4

Step 5

Step 6

≷ done ≷

draw
it!

line drawing: cacti & succulents

saguaro

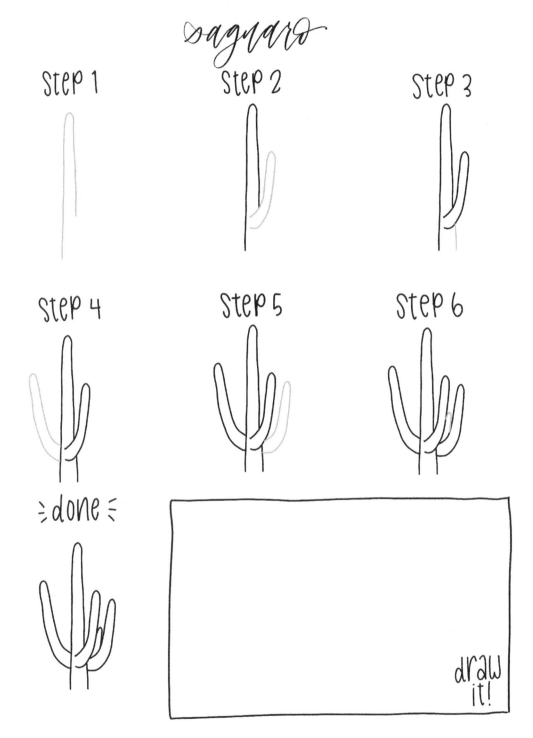

step 1

step 2

step 3

step 4

step 5

step 6

≥ done ≤

draw it!

ballerina flower

step 1

step 2

step 3

step 4

step 5

step 6

﹦ done ﹦

draw it!

line drawing: cacti & succulents

ball cactus

step 1

step 2

step 3

step 4

step 5
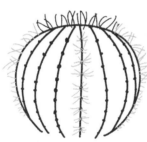

step 6

≷ done ≷
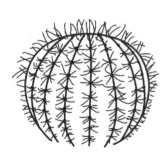

draw it!

african queen of the night

step 1

step 2

step 3

step 4

step 5

step 6

⋛ done ⋚

draw it!

line drawing: cacti & succulents
tuna cardona

step 1

step 2

step 3

step 4

step 5

step 6

≥ done ≥

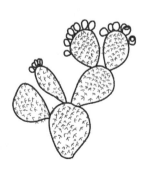

draw it!

pencil tongue

step 1

step 2

step 3

step 4

step 5

step 6

≥ done ≤

draw it!

78

peyote

step 1

step 2

step 3

step 4

step 5

step 6

≋ done ≋

draw
it!

line drawing: cacti & succulents

ruby ball cactus

Step 1

Step 2

Step 3

Step 4

Step 5

Step 6

done

draw it!

80

organ pipe cactus

Step 1

Step 2

Step 3

Step 4

Step 5

Step 6

≥ done ≤

draw
it!

jumping cholla

step 1

step 2

step 3

step 4

step 5

step 6

≥ done ≥

draw
it!

line drawing: cacti & succulents

peanut cactus

step 1

step 2

step 3

step 4

step 5

step 6

≷ done ≷

draw it!

orchid cactus

step 1

step 2

step 3

step 4

step 5

step 6

⋛done⋚

draw
it!

pincushion cactus

step 1

step 2

step 3

step 4

step 5

step 6

≶ done ≷

draw it!

rat tail cactus

step 1

step 2

step 3

step 4

step 5

step 6

≥ done ≤

draw
it!

myrtle cactus

step 1

step 2

step 3

step 4

step 5

step 6

≥ done ≤

draw
it!

line drawing: cacti & succulents
old lady cactus

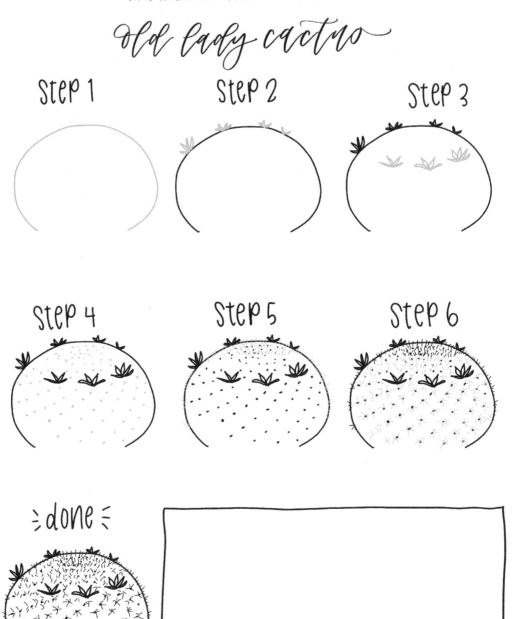

step 1

step 2

step 3

step 4

step 5

step 6

≥ done ≤

draw it!

paper spine cactus

step 1

step 2

step 3

step 4

step 5

step 6

≥ done ≤

draw it!

claret cup cactus

Step 1

Step 2

Step 3

Step 4

Step 5

Step 6

≥ done ≤

draw it!

emerald idol

STEP 1

STEP 2

STEP 3

STEP 4

STEP 5

STEP 6

≥ done ≤

draw it!

dumpling cactus

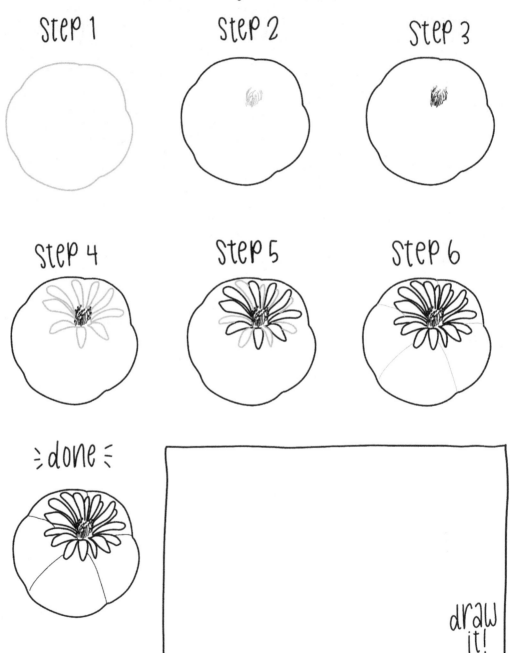

step 1

step 2

step 3

step 4

step 5

step 6

≥ done ≤

draw it!

line drawing: cacti & succulents
golden star

step 1

step 2

step 3

step 4

step 5

step 6

≷ done ≷

draw
it!

cardon cactus

step 1

step 2

step 3

step 4

step 5

step 6

⋛ done ⋛

draw it!

line drawing: cacti & succulents

fishbone cactus

step 1

step 2

step 3

step 4

step 5

step 6

≥ done ≤

draw it!

line drawing: cacti & succulents

irish mittens

step 1

step 2

step 3

step 4

step 5

step 6

done

draw it!

line drawing: cacti & succulents

joshua tree

STEP 1

STEP 2

STEP 3

STEP 4

STEP 5

STEP 6

≋ done ≋

draw it!

bunny ears

Step 1

Step 2

Step 3

Step 4

Step 5

Step 6

≥ done ≤

draw it!

crown cactus

step 1

step 2

step 3

step 4

step 5

step 6

≥ done ≤

draw it!

line drawing: cacti & succulents

hatchet cactus

step 1

step 2

step 3

step 4

step 5
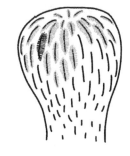

step 6

≷ done ≷

draw it!

hedgehog cactus

step 1

step 2

step 3

step 4

step 5

step 6

ξ done ξ

draw it!

line drawing: cacti & succulents

barrel cactus

step 1

step 2

step 3
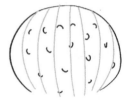

step 4

step 5

step 6

≥ done ≥

draw it!

line drawing: cacti & succulents
cob cactus

step 1

step 2

step 3

step 4

step 5

step 6

≥ done ≤

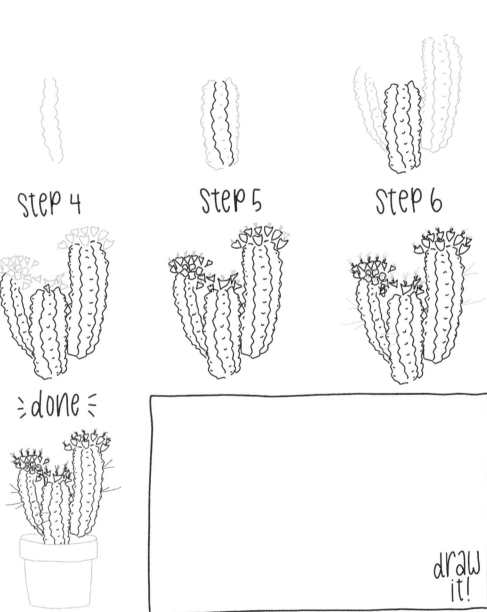

draw it!

line drawing: cacti & succulents

christmas cactus

step 1

step 2

step 3

step 4

step 5

step 6

≥ done ≤

draw it!

line drawing: cacti & succulents

endian fig

step 1

step 2

step 3

step 4

step 5

step 6

≥ done ≥

draw it!

line drawing: cacti & succulents

mexican lime cactus

step 1

step 2

step 3

step 4

step 5

step 6

≳ done ≲

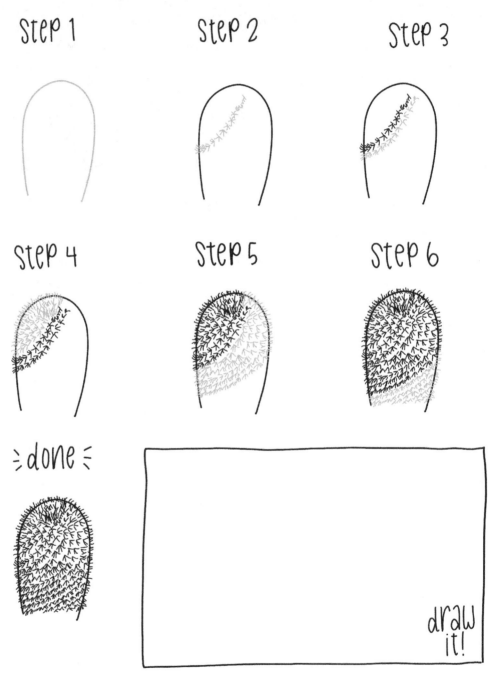

draw
it!

line drawing: cacti & succulents

moon cactus

step 1

step 2

step 3

step 4

step 5

step 6

⸝done⸜

draw
it!

line drawing: cacti & succulents
texas nipple cactus

step 1

step 2

step 3

step 4

step 5

step 6

≥ done ≤

draw it!

line drawing: cacti & succulents

club cactus

step 1

step 2

step 3

step 4

step 5

step 6

≷ done ≷

draw
it!

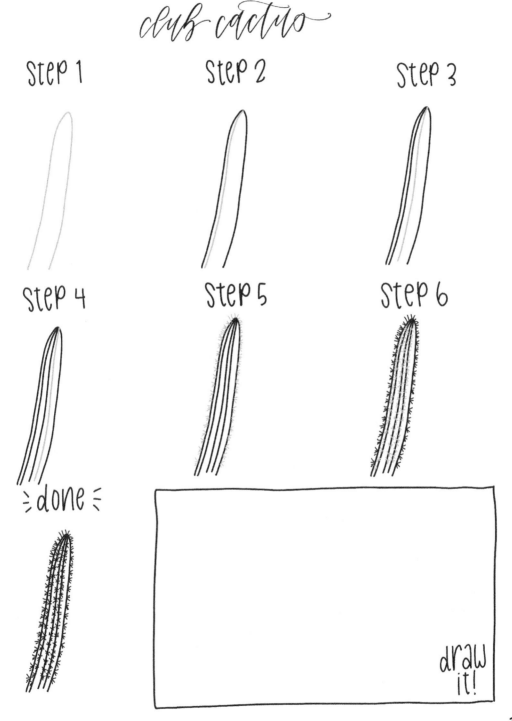

109

succulents

redbird

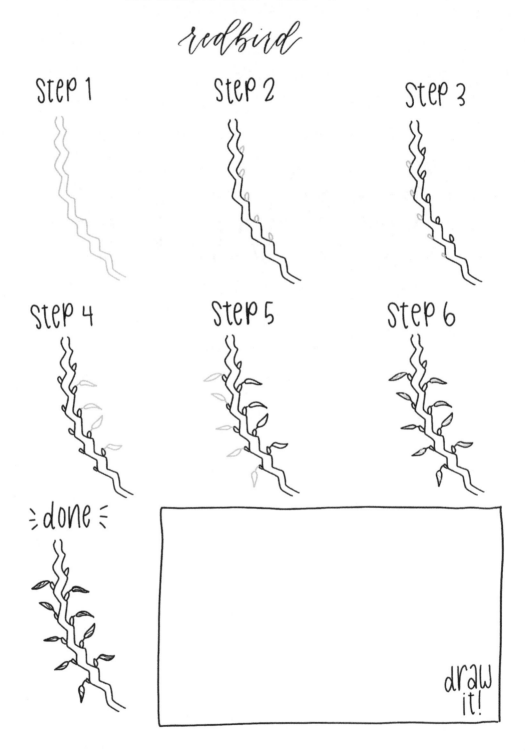

step 1

step 2

step 3

step 4

step 5

step 6

≳ done ≲

draw it!

desert spoon

step 1

step 2

step 3

step 4

step 5

step 6

⋛ done ⋚

draw it!

sea squill

step 1

step 2

step 3

step 4

step 5

step 6

≷ done ≷

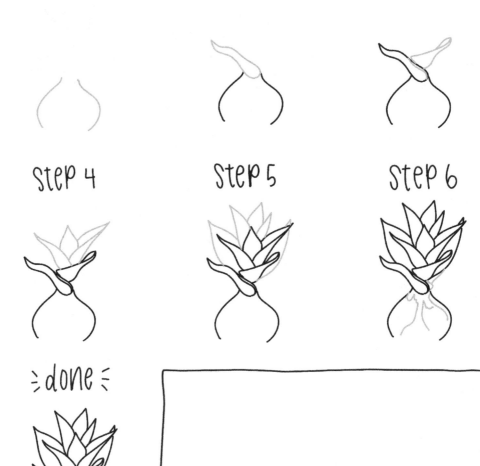

draw
it!

line drawing: cacti & succulents

oregon stonecrop

step 1

step 2

step 3

step 4

step 5

step 6

≋ done ≋

draw
it!

madagascar palm

step 1

step 2

step 3

step 4

step 5

step 6

≷done≷

draw
it!

zebra plant

step 1

step 2

step 3

step 4

step 5

step 6

≥ done ≤

draw it!

propeller plant

step 1

step 2

step 3

step 4

step 5

step 6

≋ done ≋

draw it!

boojum tree

step 1

step 2

step 3

step 4

step 5

step 6

≥ done ≤

draw
it!

line drawing: cacti & succulents

pencil plant

Step 1

Step 2

Step 3

Step 4

Step 5

Step 6

≶ done ≶

draw it!

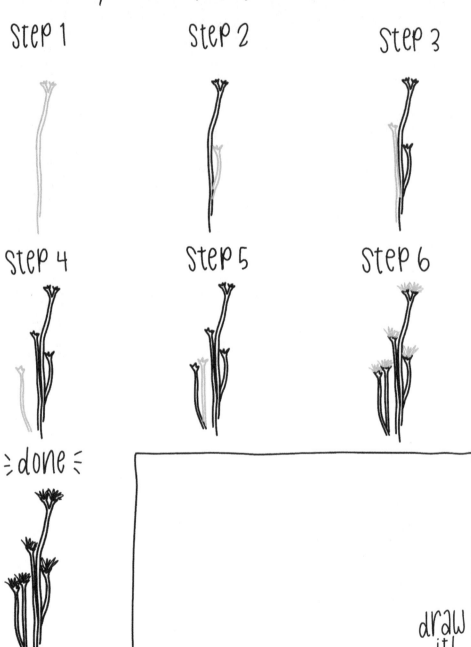

grendelion

step 1

step 2

step 3

step 4

step 5

step 6

≥ done ≤

draw
it!

yucca palm

step 1

step 2

step 3

step 4

step 5

step 6

≋ done ≋

draw it!

line drawing: cacti & succulents

dragon's bones cactus

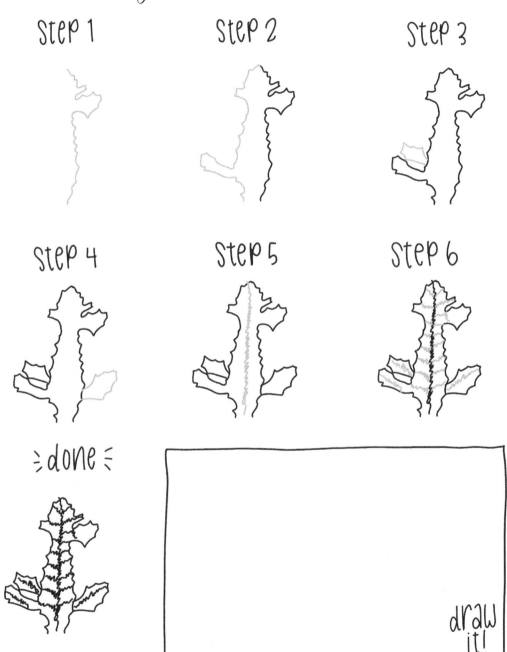

step 1

step 2

step 3

step 4

step 5

step 6

≥ done ≤

draw it!

line drawing: cacti & succulents

showy dewflower

step 1

step 2

step 3

step 4

step 5

step 6

≥ done ≤

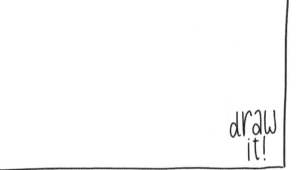

draw it!

lime lily

step 1

step 2

step 3

step 4

step 5

step 6

÷ done ÷

draw it!

line drawing: cacti & succulents
scarlet kleinia

step 1   **step 2**   **step 3**

step 4   **step 5**   **step 6**

⋲ done ⋺

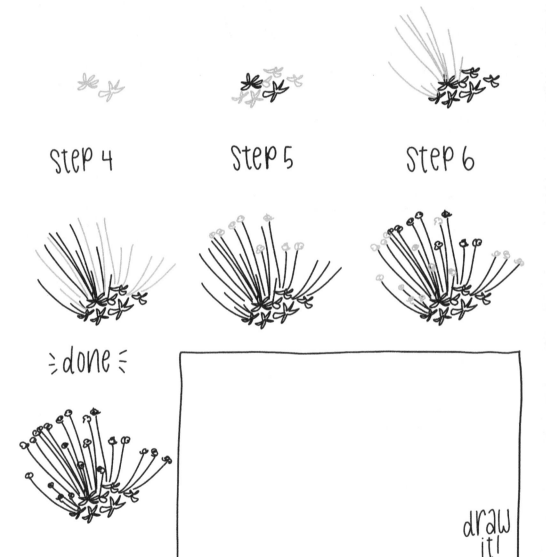

draw
it!

scarlet paintbrush

step 1

step 2

step 3

step 4

step 5

step 6

≥ done ≤

draw it!

line drawing: cacti & succulents
and lettuce

step 1

step 2

step 3

step 4

step 5

step 6

done

draw it!

line drawing: cacti & succulents

saucer plant

step 1

step 2

step 3

step 4

step 5

step 6

≥ done ≤

draw it!

crown of thorns

step 1

step 2

step 3

step 4

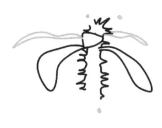

step 5

step 6

≥ done ≤

draw it!

line drawing: cacti & succulents

horombe clubfoot

step 1

step 2

step 3

step 4

step 5

step 6

≥ done ≤

draw
it!

line drawing: cacti & succulents

baby sun rose

step 1   **step 2**   **step 3**

step 4   **step 5**   **step 6**

> done >

draw
it!

132

bottleplant shrub

step 1

step 2

step 3

step 4

step 5

step 6

≥ done ≤

draw it!

133

line drawing: cacti & succulents

impala lily

step 1

step 2

step 3

step 4

step 5

step 6

done

draw it!

walking kalanchoe

step 1

step 2

step 3

step 4

step 5

step 6

≥ done ≥

draw it!

zimbabwe aloe

step 1

step 2

step 3

step 4

step 5

step 6

≈ done ≈

draw it!

zanzibar gem

Step 1

Step 2

Step 3

Step 4

Step 5

Step 6

≷ done ≷

draw
it!

line drawing: cacti & succulents

octopus agave

step 1

step 2

step 3

step 4

step 5

step 6

≈ done ≈

draw it!

line drawing: cacti & succulents

octopus plant

step 1

step 2

step 3

step 4

step 5

step 6

≥ done ≥

draw it!

chain plant

step 1

step 2

step 3

step 4

step 5

step 6

≷ done ≷

draw it!

starfish plant

step 1

step 2

step 3

step 4

step 5

step 6

⋛ done ⋚

draw it!

aloe vera

step 1

step 2

step 3

step 4

step 5

step 6

≥ done ≤

draw it!

fang

step 1

step 2

step 3

step 4

step 5

step 6

≥ done ≤

draw it!

lewisia

step 1

step 2

step 3

step 4

step 5

step 6

≷ done ≷

draw it!

line drawing: cacti & succulents

wax plant

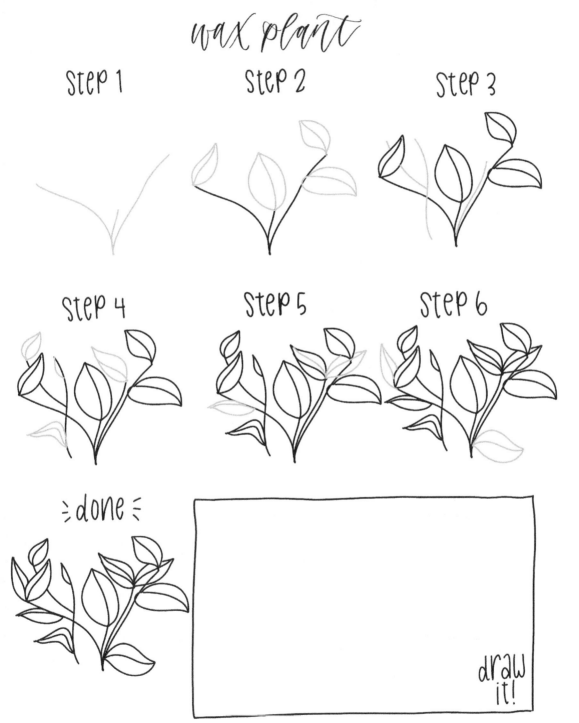

step 1

step 2

step 3

step 4

step 5

step 6

≳ done ≲

draw it!

hoodia

step 1

step 2

step 3

step 4

step 5

step 6

≥ done ≥

draw it!

line drawing: cacti & succulents

chocolate soldier

step 1

step 2

step 3

step 4

step 5

step 6

≷ done ≷

draw it!

line drawing: cacti & succulents
white vygie

step 1

step 2

step 3

step 4

step 5

step 6

done

draw it!

line drawing: cacti & succulents

green rose

step 1

step 2

step 3

step 4

step 5

step 6

≥ done ≤

draw it!

line drawing: cacti & succulents

hens & chicks

step 1

step 2

step 3

step 4

step 5

step 6

≷ done ≷

draw it!

line drawing: cacti & succulents

spanish dagger

STEP 1

STEP 2

STEP 3

STEP 4

STEP 5

STEP 6

≥ done ≤

draw it!

line drawing: cacti & succulents
october daphne

step 1

step 2

step 3

step 4

step 5

step 6

⋛ done ⋚

draw
it!

dwarf stonecrop

step 1

step 2

step 3

step 4

step 5

step 6

≥ done ≥

draw it!

line drawing: cacti & succulents

lion's tail

step 1

step 2

step 3

step 4

step 5

step 6

≽ done ≼

draw
it!

line drawing: cacti & succulents

lavender scallop

step 1

step 2

step 3

step 4

step 5

step 6

≥ done ≥

draw it!

life saver plant

step 1

step 2

step 3

step 4

step 5

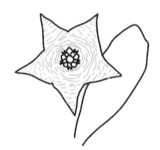

step 6

≋ done ≋

draw it!

line drawing: cacti & succulents

sisal

Step 1

Step 2

Step 3

Step 4

Step 5

Step 6

≳done≲

draw it!

rattlesnake tail

Step 1

Step 2

Step 3

Step 4

Step 5

Step 6

⋛ done ⋚

draw
it!

158

horse's teeth

step 1

step 2

step 3

step 4

step 5

step 6

≶done≶

draw it!

orange star

step 1

step 2

step 3

step 4

step 5

step 6

⋛ done ⋛

draw it!

line drawing: cacti & succulents

crocus

step 1

step 2

step 3

step 4

step 5

step 6

≥ done ≤

draw it!

line drawing: cacti & succulents

plush plant

Step 1

Step 2

Step 3

step 4

step 5

step 6

≷ done ≷

draw it!

line drawing: cacti & succulents

hottentot fig

step 1

step 2

step 3

step 4

step 5

step 6

ꞏdoneꞏ

draw it!

line drawing: cacti & succulents
leaky umbrella

step 1

step 2

step 3

step 4

step 5

step 6

≷ done ≷

draw it!

line drawing: cacti & succulents

fame flower

step 1

step 2

step 3

step 4

step 5

step 6

≷done≷

draw it!

line drawing: cacti & succulents

living stone

STEP 1

STEP 2

STEP 3

STEP 4

STEP 5

STEP 6

≥ done ≤

draw it!

line drawing: cacti & succulents

grass aloe

step 1

step 2

step 3

step 4

step 5

step 6

≥ done ≤

draw it!

line drawing: cacti & succulents

calico hearts

step 1

step 2

step 3

step 4

step 5

step 6

≥ done ≤

draw it!

maroon chenille plant

step 1

step 2

step 3

step 4

step 5

step 6

⋛ done ⋚

draw it!

spiral grass

step 1

step 2

step 3

step 4

step 5

step 6

⋛ done ⋚

draw it!

line drawing: cacti & succulents

little warty

step 1

step 2

step 3

step 4

step 5

step 6

≥done≥

draw it!

line drawing: cacti & succulents

kambroo

step 1

step 2

step 3

step 4

step 5

step 6

≥ done ≥

draw
it!

line drawing: cacti & succulents

ice plant

step 1

step 2

step 3

step 4

step 5

step 6

≥ done ≤

draw
it!

cobweb houseleek

step 1

step 2

step 3

step 4

step 5

step 6

≥done≥

draw it!

line drawing: cacti & succulents

cabbage on a stick

step 1

step 2

step 3

step 4

step 5

step 6

done

draw it!

moonstone

step 1

step 2

step 3

step 4

step 5

step 6

⋛ done ⋚

draw
it!

line drawing: cacti & succulents

string of pearls

step 1

step 2

step 3

step 4

step 5

step 6

≥ done ≤

draw it!

line drawing: cacti & succulents

Buddha's temple

step 1

step 2

step 3

step 4

step 5

step 6

≳ done ≲

draw
it!

line drawing: cacti & succulents

spiny aloe

step 1

step 2

step 3

step 4

step 5

step 6

≷done≷

draw it!

line drawing: cacti & succulents

golden carpet

step 1

step 2

step 3

step 4

step 5

step 6

÷ done ÷

draw it!

stonecrop

step 1

step 2

step 3

step 4

step 5

step 6

≥ done ≤

draw
it!

line drawing: cacti & succulents

bear grass

step 1

step 2

step 3

step 4

step 5

step 6

≑ done ≑

draw it!

line drawing: cacti & succulents

tom thumb

step 1

step 2

step 3

step 4

step 5

step 6

≥ done ≤

draw it!

rosary vine

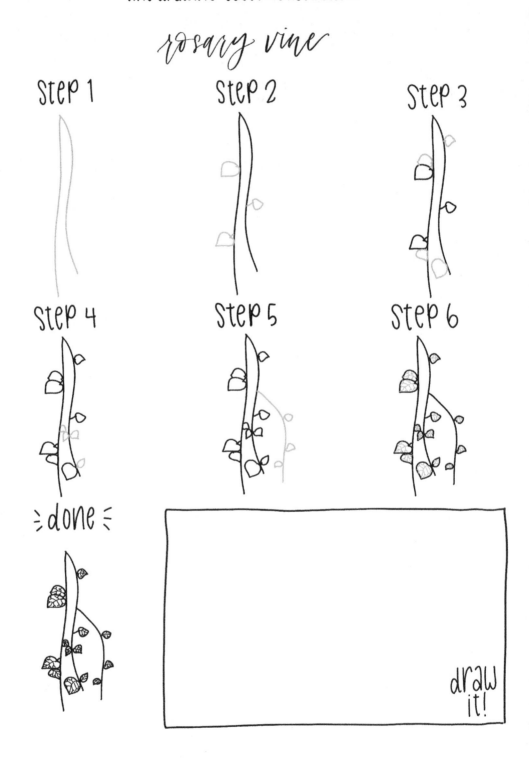

step 1

step 2

step 3

step 4

step 5

step 6

done

draw
it!

line drawing: cacti & succulents

purolane

step 1

step 2

step 3

step 4

step 5

step 6

≥ done ≤

draw it!

arabian wax cissus

step 1

step 2

step 3

step 4

step 5

step 6

≥ done ≥

draw it!

line drawing: cacti & succulents

plover egg plant

step 1 **step 2** **step 3**

step 4 **step 5** **step 6**

≷ done ≷

draw it!

panda plant

step 1

step 2

step 3

step 4

step 5

step 6

≥ done ≤

draw it!

line drawing: cacti & succulents

paddle plant

Step 1

Step 2

Step 3

Step 4

Step 5

Step 6

≡ done ≡

draw it!

moss rose

step 1   **step 2**   **step 3**

step 4   **step 5**   **step 6**

≷done≷

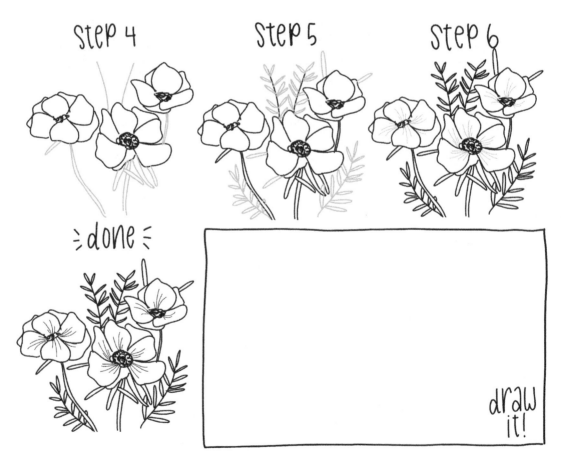

draw it!

line drawing: cacti & succulents

necklace vine

step 1

step 2

step 3

step 4

step 5

step 6

⸮ done ⸮

draw it!

line drawing: cacti & succulents

voilet queen

Step 1

Step 2

Step 3

Step 4

Step 5

Step 6

≥ done ≤

draw it!

line drawing: cacti & succulents

karoo rose

Step 1

Step 2

Step 3

Step 4

Step 5

Step 6

≥ done ≤

draw it!

milk bush

step 1

step 2

step 3

step 4

step 5

step 6

⟩ done ⟨

draw
it!

194

line drawing: cacti & succulents

jade plant

step 1

step 2

step 3

step 4

step 5

step 6

≷ done ≷

draw it!

line drawing: cacti & succulents

inchworm plant

step 1

step 2

step 3

step 4

step 5

step 6

≥ done ≤

draw it!

line drawing: cacti & succulents
fan aloe

step 1   **step 2**   **step 3**

step 4   **step 5**   **step 6**

≷ done ≷

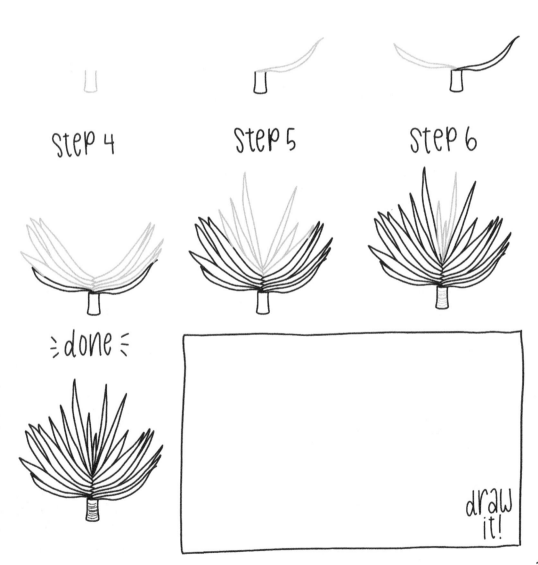

draw
it!

hoary navelwort

step 1

step 2

step 3

step 4

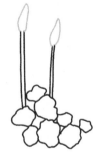

step 5

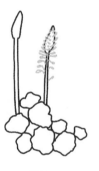

step 6

≥ done ≥

draw it!

line drawing: cacti & succulents
ghost plant

step 1

step 2

step 3

step 4

step 5

step 6

≷ done ≷

draw it!

line drawing: cacti & succulents
coral aloe

STEP 1

STEP 2

STEP 3

STEP 4

STEP 5

STEP 6

≷ done ≷

draw it!

cape blanco

Step 1

Step 2

Step 3

Step 4

Step 5

Step 6

≥ done ≥

draw it!

line drawing: cacti & succulents

fairy washboard

STEP 1

STEP 2

STEP 3

STEP 4

STEP 5

STEP 6

⋛ done ⋚

draw it!

line drawing: cacti & succulents
cocoon plant

step 1

step 2

step 3

step 4

step 5

step 6

≥ done ≤

draw it!

chalk rose

step 1

step 2

step 3

step 4

step 5

step 6

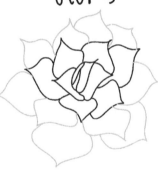

⋛ done ⋛

draw it!

candle plant

step 1

step 2

step 3

step 4

step 5

step 6

≥ done ≤

draw it!

line drawing: cacti & succulents

botterboom

step 1   step 2   step 3

step 4   step 5   step 6

≷ done ≷

draw it!

snake plant

step 1

step 2

step 3

step 4

step 5

step 6

≥ done ≤

draw it!

baby toes

step 1

step 2

step 3

step 4

step 5

step 6

≥ done ≤

draw it!

line drawing: cacti & succulents

agave

step 1

step 2

step 3

step 4

step 5

step 6

≥ done ≤

draw it!

burro tail

Step 1

Step 2

Step 3

Step 4

Step 5

Step 6

≥ done ≤

draw it!

line drawing: cacti & succulents

air plant

step 1

step 2

step 3

step 4

step 5

step 6

≥ done ≥

draw
it!

About Peggy

hello

I'M → THESE

Author
hand letterer
illustrator
painter
instructor
platform Artist
DiYer

PUBLISHED HERE

Style Me Pretty
White Mag
hochzeitswahn
Smitten Magazine
Oregon Bride Magazine

PACIFIC NORTHWEST GROWN
est. 1986

these are a few of my favorite things

SLIPPERS   BOHEMIAN DECOR
MERMAIDS   WILD FLOWERS
SODA WATER   EVERY SINGLE ANIMAL
NINTENDO   PLAYDOH
CANDLES   PRECIOUS STONES
BUBBLES   CHOCOLATE PUDDING
SWEATERS   HOUSEPLANTS
TRAVEL

DISCOVER ADDITIONAL TIPS, DIY PROJECTS, ONLINE WATCH-AT-YOUR-LEISURE CLASSES, ART FOR PURCHASE, AND A PLETHORA OF MORE PRACTICE SHEETS BY VISITING

the blog

www.thePiGeonLetters.com

GRAB MY OTHER BOOKS →

the ultimate brush lettering guide
botanical line drawing

the pigeon letters

INDEX

Made in the USA
Las Vegas, NV
16 March 2024

87299337R00122